DIEGO

Bigger Than Life

Carmen T. Bernier-Grand

Illustrated by David Diaz

Marshall Cavendish Children

To Becky, Carolyn, David, Dorothy, Ellen, Eric, Pam, Margaret, Susan, and Winnie for their help with painting this mural of words.
—C.T.B-G.

For Sarah
—D.D.

Acknowledgments

The paintings in this book are used by permission and through the courtesy of: Pg. 23, *Jacques Lipchitz (Portrait of a Young Man)*, Paris 1914 and Pg. 33, *Flower Festival: Feast of Santa Anita*, 1931. Digital Image © The Museum of Modern Art/Licensed by SCALA/Art Resource, NY © 2009, Banco de Mexico Diego Rivera & Frida Kahlo Museums Trust, Av. Cinco de mayo No. 2 Col. Central, Del. Cuauhtemoc 06059, Mexico, D.F., Pg. 34, *The Land's Bounty Rightfuly Possessed*, 1926–27 and Pg. 52, *The Watermelons*, 1957, Fundacion Dolores Olmedo, Mexico City, D.F., Mexico. Schalkwijk/Art Resource, NY © 2009, Banco de Mexico Diego Rivera & Frida Kahlo Museums Trust, Av. Cinco de mayo No. 2 Col. Centro, Del. Cuauhtemoc 06059, Mexico, D.F., Pg. 53, Diego Rivera, Undated photograph. ©2008, The Josef and Anni Albers Foundation/Artists Rights Society (ARS), New York/ Art Resource, NY.

Marshall Cavendish Corporation, 99 White Plains Road, Tarrytown, NY 10591
www.marshallcavendish.us/kids

Library of Congress Cataloging-in-Publication Data
Bernier-Grand, Carmen T.
Diego: bigger than life / by Carmen T. Bernier-Grand ; illustrated by David Diaz.—1st ed.
p. cm.
Summary: "The life and work of the artist Diego Rivera is told through chronological poems that capture salient points in his life"--Provided by publisher.
Includes bibliographical references.
ISBN 978-0-7614-5383-3 (alk. paper)
1. Rivera, Diego, 1886-1957—Juvenile literature.
2. Painters—Mexico—Biography—Juvenile literature. I. Diaz, David. II. Title.
CURR ND259.R5B47 2009   759.972—dc22   [B]   2007013761

The illustrations are rendered in mixed media.
Book design by Patrice Sheridan
Editor: Margery Cuyler

Printed in the United States of America
First edition
3 5 6 4 2

CONTENTS

FABULOUS STORYTELLER

What is life but a story?
I choose to embellish my life story.

I am DIEGO—
the charming, monstrous,
caring, hideous
Mexican muralist.

SINGING FROGS

I was born
—feet first—
December 8, 1886,
in a Mexican town whose name sounds
like singing frogs in water:
Guanajuato.

So pale and dead I looked
that the midwife dumped me
in a dung bucket;
then helped my frail mother
give birth to my twin brother,
José Carlos María.

Tía Cesaria picked me up,
eased me to the warm breast
of my Indian wet nurse:
Antonia.

MY TWIN BROTHER

When I was one and a half,
Mamá knelt and wailed by a tomb.

Feathery faint,
I waited for my twin brother to awake
from his long siesta.

Papá told Antonia to take me to the sierra.
Herbs and magic rites
would keep me from dying too.

ANTONIA THE HEALER

On a burro I rode to the sierra,
and Antonia gave me a goat.
I roamed freely, breathing fresh air,
trusting jaguars, and loving Antonia.
Her Tarascan Indian melodies lulled me to sleep.

Walking with her braided head held high,
Antonia showed me
how the rocks looked small from far away,
large as we moved closer.

We lay flat on the humid soil.
She told me that turquoise stars,
opal stars, silver stars sometimes
looped together to crown
good boys who died
and good boys who lived.

We returned home when I was four.
I was no longer scrawny,
but a fat frog with bulging, eager eyes.

THE ENGINEER

I drew on furniture, walls, floors.
I drew pulleys, wheels, gears
in the margins and between the lines
of Papá's best books.

Papá took me to a room—
black cloth on the walls and floor,
a canvas for me to paint!

I chalked an engine,
its large chimney blowing out smoke.

I drew a boxcar like a giant shoe,
a caboose like a house.

The whistle blew,
the bell clanged,
the locomotive chugged along the tracks.

DEVIL DIEGO

Tía Vicenta took me
to Templo San Diego de Alcalá.
Lush incense scent.
Votive candles burning in rows.
A woman, her head covered by a black *rebozo*,
praying a rosary of watermelon seeds.
Wall paintings of white, fat winged babies.

Tía Vicenta asked me to kneel and pray
to the statue of the Virgin Mary.
I snorted in disgust.
"She's made out of balsa wood.
Her ears have no holes to hear me."

Fingers of women twitched,
making the sign of the cross.
"The devil is in him!"

THE SOUND OF LIFE

When I was five, I yearned for a brother.
Instead, my sister, María del Pilar, was born.
Two years later, we moved to Mexico City.
Mamá wanted me to go
to a school run by the Church.
Papá wanted me to go
to a military school.

Tall and fat,
I saw myself dressed like a priest,
then a soldier.
I laughed out loud.

I went to a school run by the Church,
then another, and another.
A French teacher
spoke to me about a world without
rich people or poor people, only equals.
And Father Servín admired the pastel landscapes
I painted under a petroleum lamp.
He told me to be whatever I wanted to be.

I thought of myself in overalls,
heart-shaped palette in hand,
paintbrush dripping the vivid red Indians liked.
Artist had the sacred sound of life.

ON THE ROAD TO BECOMING AN ARTIST

The clink-clink sound of the press
and the sweet smell of hot black ink—
José Guadalupe Posada's engraving shop.
I pressed my nose against the window's dirty pane.
Zinc engravings of bandits, the latest train wreck,
the sun blazing in the night sky—
everything expressed through the force of feeling.
An etching of *La Catrina*, a grinning skeleton dressed
like the women who strolled on Sunday afternoons
in the shade of the poplars of the Alameda Park,
a park where the police kept out the Indians.

I knew then the only road I must travel.

Saying I was thirteen instead of ten,
I enrolled in night classes as a non-degree student
at the San Carlos Royal Academy of Fine Arts.
I received the second prize in drawing
and a scholarship to study art by day.
My classmates, older than I was,
laughed at my shocking-pink socks, my short pants,
the wiggly frogs peering out of my pockets.
I earned the highest grades and every possible art prize.

PASSAGE OF ANGER

Nineteen years old, a hair over six feet tall
and three hundred pounds,
I was given a scholarship
to study art in La Madre España.
Waiting for the ship to Spain in Veracruz,
I saw mill owners
treating workers like beasts:
long hours, miserable wages.
Peasants
walking out of the mills.
Foremen
hitting Indian strikers.
I cried silently.

The workers appealed
to President Porfirio Díaz,
the "Father of His People."
I wanted to join them, but even brave men
get scared of terror.
President Porfirio Díaz
sent out troops.
Shooting!
Dead Indians,
piled on railway flatcars,
thrown into the harbor.

I boarded the ship bound for
Spain to study art
paid for by a tyrant's
government.
I stood at the bow, screaming!

NO MORE CÉZANNES

Something was missing in Mexico.
Something was missing in Spain.
I went to France.
In Paris I stood outside a gallery
that had Cézanne's painting in its window,
a peasant smoking a pipe.
I saw him moving,
I saw him tranquil,
I saw him glancing at me.
From time to time,
the shop owner also glanced at me.
At lunch, he made sure the door was locked.
On his way back, he found me rooted to the same spot.
He replaced the painting with Cézanne's *Card Players*:

Card player sitting straight, wearing
purple tall hat, purple jacket,
yellow pants

Card player hunching forward, wearing
yellow scrunched-down hat, yellow jacket,
purple pants

The shop owner brought more Cézannes to the window.

After dusk, he opened the door. "I have no more."
It was then I felt the rain that had drenched me.

DIEGO DIEGOVICH

I caught Russian artist Angelina Beloff on my canvas:
azure aura, head slightly tilted, sapphire eyes.
She wrapped herself in a finely woven black wool shawl,
sat away from me.
"My love for you is much greater than your indifference,"
I said in French, our only common language.

I admired her country, Vladimir Lenin, Leon Trotsky,
and their socialist beliefs.
She mocked them. "Our country is so backward!"

Picking wildflowers for her, I fell into a canal.
She held in her laughter,
shook the water off the flowers, placed them by her chest.
We became lovers,
until she saw my protest painting of Notre Dame.
"Diego Diegovich,
I foresee certain complications in our lives.
For that reason, I've decided
to take a closer look at our relationship."

She left "to reflect in peace."
I sailed to Mexico,
sure I would return to Paris to hear my fate.

THE MEXICAN REVOLUTION

Mexico City,
where the Revolution was not happening,
where no Mexicans died,
where I sold my paintings
to President Porfirio Díaz's wife.

A bomb ticked in my heart.
Generations of Indian children,
shivering, thirsting, starving,
could accuse me of treason.

This tale I told:
That my plot to kill Porfirio Díaz failed
when his wife, not he, attended my exhibit.
That I went to the south of Mexico,
where the Revolution *was* happening.
That I blew up trains and rode the revolutionary hills
with Emiliano Zapata.
That a trusted coachman warned me to leave Mexico
to escape Porfirio Díaz's firing squad.

In truth, I made sure that the government would continue
to pay my art scholarship, and I boarded a ship to Europe—
a storm of guilt almost sank me in mid-ocean.

BEHOLD THE ANGEL

In April, I telegrammed Angelina:
Heading for Paris!
In May, I disembarked in Santander,
visited friends in Madrid,
detoured to an international art exposition in Barcelona,
sent no word to Angelina of my whereabouts.
In June, I finally arrived in Paris.
As soon as I looked into Angelina's eyes
—full of light as if blue had dripped from the sky—
I slipped a ring on her finger.
I loved my mate,
like her name,
truly angelical.

MEXICAN CUBISM

Cubism

    broke

        down

            forms,

used the p i e c e s to create new worlds:

triangles, circles, squares, rectangles.

        My friend Pablo Picasso—

      the greatest cubist in the world.

    I never believed in God, but I believed in Picasso.

     Critics said my Mexican cubism was interesting.

       I could live on it. The rich bought it.

      It hung where the poor couldn't afford to go.

        That wasn't what I wanted.

          I resigned cubism.

Jacques Lipchitz (Portrait of a Young Man) by Diego Rivera, Paris 1914. Oil on canvas. *In 1912, cubist sculptor Jacques Lipchitz joined a group of artists that included Pablo Picasso and Diego Rivera.*

WORLD WAR I BABY

I painted Angelina with her sun-round belly.
"If the child disturbs me," I told her,
"I'll throw it out the window."
Angelina's smile disappeared,
tears not yet formed but forming.
What made me say that?
Was the devil in me?

I painted Angelina breast-feeding Dieguito.
He was trembling under a threadbare blanket.
Lack of food, firewood, and coal due to the war.
It was cold, bitterly cold.
Pipes froze. Throaty cries.
Dieguito's fever burned a hole in my heart.
I ran down the stairs, into the street.
I was thirty-one, and I couldn't support my family.
I came to Europe, looking for a style I couldn't find.
I couldn't return to corrupt Mexico.
I'd taken money from the government I objected to.
I was a traitor!
I was a failure!

In his mother's arms, Dieguito died.
I wept.

GOOD-BYES

Angelina's grief was as silent as the moon.
We hardly spoke or touched.
I loved love more than I loved her.
Good-bye, Angelina.

I left for Italy,
studied the Byzantine mosaics,
the frescoes with white, fat-winged babies,
tomb paintings
telling the stories of the dead,
tales like we told in Mexico.

I was being pulled to Mexico.
Peasants and workers
had overthrown Porfirio Díaz.
The new government believed
in education and the arts.
My wretched and exuberant country was ready
for my ardent imagination.
Good-bye, Europe.

SAVAGE BEAUTY

The strange creature moved slowly, precisely, intensely.
Her hair looked more like that of a chestnut mare than a woman's,
her green eyes so transparent she seemed to be blind.
She gazed at my sketches for *The Creation,*
a mural with too many Italian halos.
Not Mexican enough.
I was imitating—again!

The wild filly inclined her wild mane.
"Is *this* the great Diego Rivera?
To me, he looks horrible!"

Her hands ripped off a banana from the fruit bowl,
hands with the beauty of roots or eagle talons.
Her full lips opened,
the corners drooping like those of a tiger.
She threw the banana skin against the wall.
Animal teeth set in coral like the ones in old idols
devoured the banana.
"Shall I model for you?"

Nothing could stop what would happen next:
a savage life with the beauty Lupe Marín.

TRUE MEXICO

On public walls, I'd start a social revolution.
I'd paint the poetry of the common people,
working, suffering, fighting, seeking joy, living, and dying.

To digest the tastes and scents of Mexico
in the juices of my imagination,
Lupe and I would be pilgrims up and down our land.

The whole country cried to be sketched—
fields, mines, festivals,
the works of the common people—
blown glass, textiles, jade jewelry.

I collected animals and deities molded
by Aztec hopes, fears, joys, sufferings.
Lupe called them
"horrible, expensive clay monkeys."
But they were the living heart of the true Mexico.

THE MAKING OF A FRESCO

First, I studied when and where the arches and columns broke
  the sunlight.
Then, while my assistants plastered the wall three, four times,
I sketched on paper, figures twelve feet tall.
I climbed the scaffold, made charcoal outlines of the figures.
My assistants carved them out.
Late at night they applied the last plaster coat.
By dawn, I was painting—before the plaster dried.
At the end of my working day, I climbed down the scaffold,
looked at the mural as if somebody else had painted it.
If the painting was not doing what I wanted,
I trembled, kicked, and cried—a boy having a temper tantrum.
"I'll be back tomorrow at six."

Seven days a week, eighteen hours a day,
I painted fables of the history and culture of Mexico,
  my vision of the truth,
hoping people would learn what tomorrow might look like.

BRIMMING WITH MEXICAN LIGHT

As naturally as I breathe,
I painted in grand scale the colors of Mexico—
clearer, richer, more full of light than colors in Europe.

As naturally as I speak,
I painted in grand scale the music of Mexico
in markets, crowds, festivals—
Burning of the Judases, the Dance of the Deer.

As naturally as I sweat,
I painted in grand scale the workers of Mexico
in fields, mines, streets—
Indians carrying bundles of calla lilies.

A million public walls
wouldn't be enough
to paint all the beauty of Mexico.

Flower Festival: Feast of Santa Anita by Diego Rivera, 1931. Encaustic on canvas.

The Land's Bounty Rightfully Possessed by Diego Rivera, 1926-27, Mural. Chapel. Universidad Autonoma, Chapingo, Mexico. *This is a fragment of the much larger mural. It features pregnant Lupe as* Fecund Earth.

FECUND EARTH

In my mural
in the Chapingo Chapel,
pregnant Lupe
was the model for *Fecund Earth*.

Our daughter Lupe
was born in January 1924,
her head pointy
as a mountain peak.
I called her Pico.

Our daughter Ruth
was born in June 1927,
her skin dark
as *chapopote*, tar.
I called her Chapo.

WILD WIFE

Aztec idols fed my art.
I bought red-clay puppies,
deities covered with tattoos,
goddesses breast-feeding children.

Every peso I earned with my art
I spent buying these idols.
No money left for food.

At the table, Lupe fed me
a clear broth with chopped-up pieces
of my most favorite Aztec idol!

Carrying a gray suitcase, I left for Russia.
Lupe ran after the train, yelling words of hate:
"When you come back, I won't be here."
I threw back a loud laugh, not believing her.

When I returned,
I found Lupe married to a poet.

WINGS OF A BLACKBIRD

"Diego, come down!"
Beneath my scaffold stood a young girl.
The ribbons on her crown of braids radiated light—
a feast to my eyes.
The plaster on the wall might dry,
but I climbed down from my perch.

Her dark thick eyebrows met above her nose
—wings of a blackbird.
"I want you to tell me whether you think
I can become an artist."

I followed her to the sunlit staircase.
She limped—slightly—yet
her body shimmered in the sun.

She turned three paintings to face me.
"I would appreciate your honest opinion."

I told her she must continue to paint.
Her art was as brilliant as butterflies' wings.

She invited me to see other paintings.
"I live in Coyoacán, Avenida Londres.
My name is Frida Kahlo."

DEVIL FRIDA

How come Frida
—so young, so thin, so beautiful—
allowed me
—so old, so fat, so ugly—
to court her?
Was it because I was a famous artist?

Frida's father told me that a bus accident
broke her leg in pieces
and a handrail pierced her pelvis,
like a sword through a bull.

Was it because she wanted me
to pay her medical bills?

Not wanting to let her go,
Frida's father said, "She is a devil."

Frida and I
—both devils, both artists—
married on August 21, 1929,
the happiest day of my life.

DIEGO THE RED

For seven years I had been a Red,
a member of the Mexican Communist Party,
but now I was declared unworthy of its membership.

The party argued:

I argued:

I painted in public buildings of
a non-Communist government.

I painted the walls
of public buildings for the benefit
of the poor.

I forgot party meetings and
speaking engagements.

I didn't go to meetings.
I had to paint murals while
the plaster on the walls was wet.
I served the party with my brush,
painting pictures of the life
of the toiling masses.

I didn't trust my revolutionary
fellow members.

I trusted no one.
Never could, never will.

Then the party expelled me.

I expelled myself.

AN ORCHID FOR FRIDA

To paint the pulsing rhythms
of rods and pistons
in the land of machinery and modern industry,
Frida and I went to Detroit.
Triumph for me—not for Frida.

Dieguito was a cursed name.
Once more, he wasn't meant to be.

To refresh and uplift her spirits,
I gave Frida a purple orchid.
I told her, "No more children."

She dropped the orchid.
It lay on the ground,
fading to brown.

MAN AT THE CROSSROADS

On the Rockefeller RCA building wall,
I painted a mural of my vision of hope
for a new and better future.

I painted a peasant,
who develops products from the Earth,
origin of all the riches of mankind.
I painted a worker of the cities,
who transforms and distributes
the raw materials given by the Earth.
I painted a soldier,
who represents sacrifice.
I painted them,
clasping hands with the worker's hero:
Russian leader Lenin.

A storm broke!
Mr. Nelson Rockefeller asked me
to paint out the face of Lenin.
I refused.
I was dragged away.

I returned to Mexico,
and in New York,
they hammered my mural to pieces.

VOLCANIC LOVE

Volcanic flames melt snow.
Snow puts out volcanic flames.

In volcanic Mexico, men had mistresses.
I was Mexico's son. I was what I was.
I was the lover of Cristina,
Frida's sister.
Frida said the devil was in me!

I knew that in vengeance
Frida took a lover.
The devil was in Frida!

I asked for a divorce.
She consented.

No flames. No snow. Just ashes.

ANGUISH AND TRIUMPH

Paintings full of anguish.
Everyone marveled at her talent.
Frida triumphed!

What sort of man was I?
Frida knew me.
Frida knew my art.
Frida knew my life.

Frida, like an Aztec idol,
could cost me everything,
but I had to have her.

Frida, please, stop your persistent no.
Fly to your own true love.

On my fifty-fourth birthday,
Frida and I remarried
in the city we both loved:
San Francisco.

FRIDA'S WORDS

I won't refer to Diego as my husband. Diego isn't and would never be anyone's husband. On the other hand I want to express, with the poetry I lack, what Diego really is. Diego is a social revolutionary. He has an intense desire to change the society in which he lives. Diego is a tireless artist. Always working. His capacity for energy breaks clocks and calendars. Diego is a lover of things that possess beauty. He especially loves the Indians, living flower of the cultural tradition of America. Diego is an immense baby. I'd like to always hold him in my arms.

DIEGO'S WORDS

With her beauty, swift wit, and spectacular finery
of the Indian women of Mexico,
Frida adds charm to any gathering.
I don't blame people for liking her,
because I like her too,
more than anything.

No artist in Mexico can compare with her.
Her art is acid and tender, profound and cruel.
Never has a woman painted such agonizing poetry.

Frida is
everything that interests me,
everything I love,
everything that gives meaning to my life.

DEATH DANCE

The pain that always stalked Frida
struck again.
Flesh from her foot rotted and fell off.

Leg gone.
I came home from painting all night,
watched over her as she slept.

July 13, 1954.
My beloved Frida, gone—forever!
No longer. No longer.

Life gave me time
to be with Frida more.
And I didn't take the gift.

STILL LIFES

I couldn't stand to be alone.
I couldn't take care of myself.
I couldn't even button myself.

I married my art agent, Emma Hurtado.
She flew with me to Russia to treat my cancer.
Too late. Too late.

Like Frida,
whose last painting
!Viva la vida! Long live life!
had watermelons cut open
like her, wounded like Mexico,
I painted watermelons,
a rosary of seeds praying
for my wishes to come true:
may I die in the holy ground of Mexico;
may my ashes be mixed with Frida's ashes.

The Watermelons by Diego Rivera, 1957.

EPILOGUE

On the night of November 24, 1957,
Diego died in his sleep in Mexico City.
His ashes lay in the earth
of the Rotunda of Mexico's Illustrious Men,
miles away from Frida's childhood home,
where her ashes lay.

Hence the fable of the life
of Diego Rivera ended.
The moral of the story was in the words
he once wrote to Frida:
"Take from life all it gives you."

Diego Rivera. Undated Photograph.

THE TRUE LIFE
OF DIEGO RIVERA

Diego Rivera was such a fabulous storyteller that sometimes it's difficult to discern what is true about his life. With the information available today, here are some clarifications not included in the text:

Diego Rivera (named after his father) claimed he almost died at birth. What is certain is that his mother, María del Pilar Barrientos, went into a coma after a hemorrhage giving birth to twins. Perhaps Diego told the truth when he said that a midwife attended the births, but family friend Dr. Arizmendi was definitely present. He pronounced María del Pilar dead, but the maid insisted she was still breathing. She was.

A year and a half later, the death of Diego's twin had depressed María del Pilar so much that she was incapable of caring for Diego, a thin and weak child. A family album shows photos of Diego at two, three, and four taken in a studio in Guanajuato. But Diego insisted he spent those years getting strong in the sierra with his Indian wet nurse, Antonia. In any case, during his early years, he lived among women: his mother, Aunt Cesaria, Great-aunt Vicenta, and Antonia. His sister, María, was born when he was five. When Diego was eight and María three, their baby brother, Alfonso, died.

Diego's father, a freemason, did not want his children to be raised as Catholics. But when the family moved to Mexico City in 1893, Diego attended Catholic schools at his mother's insistence. He was so smart that in third grade he was promoted to sixth grade. In 1899, following the Rivera men's tradition, he went to the National Preparatory School, where students were taught to prepare for the military academy. That lasted two weeks. Diego hated it. Instead he attended the San Carlos Royal Academy of Fine Arts.

Although Diego's father opposed the dictatorship of President Porfirio Díaz, the elder Diego worked for the government as an inspector in the National Department of Public Health. During an official trip to Veracruz in 1902, he purposely showed Diego's paintings to Governor Teodoro Dehesa. As hoped, the governor offered Diego a scholarship to study in Europe, where he painted approximately two hundred cubist works. Diego was not satisfied. Something was missing. While he had left Mexico, Mexico had not left him.

In Europe Diego met Angelina Beloff, who became his partner for ten years. While she was giving birth to Dieguito, Diego had an affair with

Russian artist Marievna Vorobiev-Stelbelska. In 1919, Marievna gave birth to Marika, whom Diego never legally recognized as his child. Marika's eyes resembled his. Intermittently throughout his life he sent Marika money.

In June 1921, Diego left Angelina in Paris to return to Mexico, saying that as soon as he had made some money he would send for her. But he never sent her money to cover the plane fare. Many years later Angelina moved to Mexico City, where she died.

In July 1921, when Diego arrived in Mexico, dictator Porfirio Díaz had been exiled to France, and the Minister of Education José Vasconcelos had initiated a program that included the creation of murals in public buildings. He offered Diego walls on which to paint murals that portrayed the cultures and traditions of Mexico. Diego had finally found his medium and style. In his lifetime he painted hundreds of acres of walls.

In 1922, Diego became a member of the Mexican Communist Party and married his favorite model, Guadalupe "Lupe" Marín, in the Catholic Church. They had two daughters who later claimed that Diego was a good father. Yet Diego and Lupe had a wild marriage. She was possessive and aggressive; he was unfaithful.

Before Diego's trip to Russia in 1927 to take part in the celebration of the tenth anniversary of the October Revolution, poet Jorge Cuesta confessed to Diego that he loved Lupe. Diego wished him good luck. Since the Mexican government did not recognize a church marriage, Diego and Lupe did not need a divorce. When Diego returned from Russia, he found Lupe had married Cuesta.

In 1929, Diego married artist Frida Kahlo. He was forty-three. She had just turned twenty-two. But as Angelina had once said, "He's just a child, a great big child." Lupe and Frida agreed.

Also in 1929, the members of the Mexican Communist Party complained that Diego had missed too many committee meetings and speaking dates. He had also accepted art commissions not only from the oppressive Mexican government but also from capitalists in the United States. Although Diego said he had expelled himself, the party expelled him. It was not until 1954, after several attempts, that Diego's application to rejoin the Mexican Communist Party was accepted.

The face of Communist Lenin in the Rockefeller Center mural in New York City was not Diego's only challenged piece. Most of his murals caused controversy. *History of the State of Morelos* in the Palace of Cortez in Cuernavaca offended many Mexicans because it was financed by American ambassador Dwight Morrow, considered to be one of the most terrible enemies of Mexico. *The Making of a Fresco* in the California School of Fine Arts (San Francisco Art Institute since 1961) was controversial because Diego included a self-portrait showing his buttocks facing the public. *Vaccination* in Detroit alienated some Christians because it showed the Holy Family vaccinating baby Jesus, although Diego never confirmed that the figures were Joseph, Mary, and Jesus. *Burlesque of Mexican Folklore and Politics* was removed from the Reforma Hotel in Mexico City because the hotel's patrons objected to the caricatures of living Mexican personalities and leading figures in world affairs. Historians objected to *Dream of a Sunday Afternoon in the Alameda Park* in Mexico City because it included the words "God does not exist." Although Diego was depressed about the removal of some of his murals, the publicity added to his fame.

It has been said that women pursued Diego more than he pursued them. He had affairs with artists, actresses, dancers, singers, and athletes. The most hurtful affair to Frida was Diego's liaison with Cristina, her youngest sister. In revenge, Frida had a brief affair with Russian leader Leon Trotsky, whom Diego had invited to Mexico. Even after Frida and Diego had reconciled, they continued to have affairs. But they loved each other. Perhaps Frida was not only Diego's wife and friend but also the mother he had yearned for.

In 1941, Diego began to build Anahuacalli, a pyramid to house his collection of about 60,000 pre-Conquest idols. When Frida died in 1954, he bequeathed the Blue House (her home in Coyoacán), Anahuacalli, and his Aztec idol collection to the Mexican people. Today the Blue House is the Frida Kahlo Museum and Anahuacalli is the Diego Rivera Museum.

A year after Frida's death, Diego married his art agent, Emma Hurtado. She accompanied him to Russia where he received cobalt treatment for cancer. On November 24, 1957, Diego died of heart failure in his sleep at his San Angel studio in Mexico City.

Although Diego Rivera did not actually fight in the Mexican Revolution, he fought a social revolution with his brush. In 1938, Leon Trotsky summarized the impact of Diego's murals: "Do you want to see with your own eyes the hidden springs of the social revolution? Look at the frescoes of Diego Rivera. Do you wish to know what revolutionary art is like? Look at the frescoes of Diego Rivera."

The history and culture of Mexico and the United States live in frescoes painted by Diego Rivera, who sought justice for the common people, especially the Indians. The Diego Rivera Foundation—founded in 2006 by his daughter Guadalupe Rivera Marín and his grandson, Diego López Rivera—is committed to encouraging people to donate walls to young artists for painting murals. May the young be allowed to paint their history, their culture, and what they believe is just in life.

—C.T.B.G.

GLOSSARY

Anahuacalli: A museum designed by Diego Rivera to house about 60,000 prehistoric Aztec pieces from his collection.

Avenida: Avenue.

Aztec: A member of a people of Central Mexico whose civilization was at its height at the time of the Spanish Conquest in the early sixteenth century.

Blue House: Frida Kahlo's childhood house, today the Frida Kahlo Museum in Coyoacán, Mexico.

Chapingo: A small town in Central Mexico.

Chapopote: Tar.

Coyoacán: A town south of Mexico City where Frida Kahlo was born.

Cubism: A school of painting and sculpture developed in Paris in the early twentieth century.

Fresco: The art of painting in fresh moist plaster.

Guanajuato: A state in Central Mexico and also the name of that state's capital city. Its Tarascan Indian name is Cuanaxhuato, "frog hill." *Cuanax* means "frog." *Huato* means "hill." Some rocks in Guanajuato look like frogs.

La Madre España: Mother Spain, the name often given to Spain after the Conquest.

Mamá: Mother. Diego's mother was María del Pilar Barrientos.

Papá: Father. Diego's father was also named Diego Rivera.

Pico: Peak.

Rebozo: Shawl.

San: Saint.

Sierra: Mountains near Guanajuato.

Tarascan: A member of a people of Southern Mexico whose civilization was at its height from the fourteenth century until the Spanish Conquest in the early sixteenth century.

Templo: Temple.

Tía: Aunt.

Veracruz: A major port city in the Gulf of Mexico.

CHRONOLOGY

1886—On December 8, José Diego María Rivera y Barrientos is born in Guanajuato, Mexico. He and his twin brother, José Carlos María Rivera y Barrientos, are the eldest children of Diego Rivera and María del Pilar Barrientos. Later Diego removes José from his name and claims that his full name is Diego María Concepción Juan Nepomuceno Estanislao Rivera y Barrientos Acosta y Rodríguez. Some biographers say Diego was imitating Picasso's long name.

1888—Diego's twin brother dies. Diego claims he is taken to the sierra where he lives more than two years with Antonia, a Tarascan Indian. Some experts say that he visits the sierra often, but lives at home.

1889—Diego begins to draw.

1891—Diego's sister, María del Pilar, is born.

1893—The Rivera-Barrientos family moves to Mexico City.

1894—Diego goes to Colegio del Padre Antonio for three months.

1895—A report card for August shows Diego attending Colegio Católico Carpenter.

1896—Diego enrolls in night courses at the San Carlos Royal Academy of Fine Arts.

1899—A report card shows Diego attending Liceo Católico Hispanic-Mexicano. Diego enrolls as a full-time student at the San Carlos Royal Academy of Fine Arts.

1905—Veracruz governor Teodoro Dehesa grants Diego a scholarship to study art in Spain.

1906—Diego shows twenty-six paintings at the annual exhibition of the San Carlos Royal Academy of Fine Arts.

1907—On January 6, Diego arrives in Spain.

1909—Diego visits France, Belgium, and England. In Brussels he meets the Russian artist Angelina Beloff and he paints her portrait.

1910—Diego exhibits at the Society of Independent Artists in Paris. He returns to Mexico in August and in November exhibits at the San Carlos Royal Academy of Fine Arts. He claims he witnesses the outbreak of the Mexican Revolution.

1911—In April or in early May, Diego arrives in Spain. In June he returns to Paris and becomes Angelina Beloff's partner for the next ten years. Cubism's influence is reflected in his work.

1913—Diego paints cubist works and exhibits at the Autumn Salon.

1914—In April, Diego has a one-man show at the Berthe Weill Gallery. He travels to Spain at the outbreak of World War I.

1915—Diego returns to Paris where he begins a relationship with the Russian artist Marievna Vorobiev-Stelbelska.

1916—In October, Diego exhibits at the Modern Gallery in New York City. His son, Diego Miguel Angel, is born to Angelina Beloff.

1917—Diego abandons cubism. In the winter, his son dies.

1918—Cézanne's influence is noticeable in Diego's work.

1919—Diego's daughter Marika is born to Marievna Vorobiev-Stelbelska.

1920—Diego travels in Italy, making numerous studies and sketches of Italian frescoes.

1921—Diego returns to Mexico City. He begins his mural *The Creation* at the National Preparatory School.

1922—In a church ceremony, Diego marries Guadalupe ("Lupe") Marín. In September, he begins the frescoes at the Ministry of Education. He co-founds the Union of Revolutionary Painters, Sculptors, and Graphic Artists and joins the Mexican Communist Party.

1924—Diego's daughter Guadalupe is born. He nicknames her Pico.

1925—While still working on the frescoes at the Ministry of Education, Diego begins to paint frescoes at the National School of Agriculture in Chapingo.

1927—Diego's daughter Ruth is born. He nicknames her Chapo. Diego and Lupe break up. In the fall, he goes to Russia to take part in the celebration of the tenth anniversary of the October Revolution.

1928—Diego returns to Mexico.

1929—On August 21, Diego marries Frida Kahlo. On October 3, the Mexican Communist Party expels Diego. He starts a mural in the National Palace that he does not finish until 1935. He also paints murals at the Ministry of Health. He is appointed director of the upper school of the San Carlos Royal Academy of Arts, but soon he is dismissed because they don't agree with his teaching policies.

1930—Diego and Frida travel to San Francisco, where he has been commissioned to paint murals at the Stock Exchange, the University of California at Berkeley, and the California School of Fine Arts (San Francisco Art Institute since 1961).

1932—Diego and Frida go to Detroit, where he has been commissioned to paint a mural for the Detroit Institute of Arts. On July 4, Frida has a miscarriage.

1933—In March, Diego and Frida arrive in New York, where he has been commissioned to paint a mural in the RCA Building. Diego includes Lenin in the mural, which results in the suspension of the project and its complete destruction after Diego and Frida return to Mexico.

1935—Diego finishes the mural in the National Palace that he started in 1929.

1936—Diego paints four frescoes in the Reforma Hotel in which he attacks Mexican political figures. The frescoes are removed.

1937—Diego receives Leon Trotsky and his wife, Natalia Sedova, in Frida Kahlo's Blue House.

1939—Diego and Trotsky's friendship disintegrates. Diego and Frida divorce.

1940—Diego paints ten murals in San Francisco for the Golden Gate International Exposition. On December 8, he remarries Frida in San Francisco.

1941—Diego begins to build Anahuacalli, a pyramid to house his collection of Aztec idols.

1943—Diego paints two murals for the National Institute of Cardiology. He is appointed professor at La Esmeralda College of Art.

1946—Diego receives a commission to paint a large mural for the new Hotel El Prado.

1947—With muralists José Clemente Orozco and David Alfaro Siqueiros, Diego forms the National Institute of Arts' Commission for Mural Painting.

1949—The fiftieth anniversary of Diego's artistic career is celebrated with a comprehensive exhibition of his works at the Palace of Fine Arts.

1950—Diego is awarded the National Prize for Plastic Arts.

1953—Diego executes a mural in glass mosaic on the facade of the Teatro de los Insurgentes. He finishes his work on the front of the Olympic Stadium on the campus of Mexico University and paints a mural in La Raza Hospital.

1954—On July 13, Frida dies in her Coyoacán house. In September, after several attempts, Diego's application to rejoin the Mexican Communist Party is accepted.

1955—On July 29, Diego marries art agent Emma Hurtado. He bequeaths Frida Kahlo's Blue House, Anahuacalli, and his pre-Columbian collection to the Mexican people. At the end of the year, he travels to Russia to undergo medical treatment for cancer.

1957—On November 24, Diego dies in his studio in San Angel, Mexico.

SOURCES

PUBLICATIONS AND TALKS

Alcántara, Isabel, and Sandra Egnolff. *Frida Kahlo and Diego Rivera.* New York: Prestel, 1999.

Brenner, Leah. *The Childhood of Diego Rivera.* New York: A. S. Barnes and Company, 1964.

Downs, Linda Bank. *Diego Rivera: The Detroit Industrial Murals.* New York: W. W. Norton & Company, 1999.

Hamill, Pete. *Diego Rivera.* New York: Harry N. Abrams, 1999.

Herrera, Hayden. *Frida: A Biography of Frida Kahlo.* New York: Perennial, 2002.

Le Clézio, J. M. G. *Diego y Frida.* Madrid: Temas de hoy, 1993.

Marnham, Patrick. *Dreaming with His Eyes Open: A Life of Diego Rivera.* Berkeley and Los Angeles: University of California Press, 2000.

Neimark, Anne E. *Diego Rivera: Artist of the People.* New York: HarperCollins Publishers, 1992.

Rivera, Diego, and Gladys March. *My Art, My Life: An Autobiography.* New York: Dover Publications, 1991.

Rivera, María del Pilar. *Mi hermano Diego.* Guanajuato, Mexico: Gobierno del Estadode Guanajuato, Secretaría de Educación Pública, 1986.

Rivera Marín, Guadalupe. *Diego Rivera the Red.* Houston: Arte Público Press, 2004.

Rivera Marín, Guadalupe, and Juan Coronel Rivera. *Encuentros con Diego Rivera.* Mexico City, Mexico: Siglo veintiuno editores, 2003.

Rivera Marín, Guadalupe. Talks at First Congregational Church and Kennedy School, Portland, Oregon, September 2005.

Rivera Marín, Guadalupe. *Un río, dos Riveras.* Mexico City, Mexico: Editorial Patria, 1989.

Tibol, Raquel. *An Open Life: Frida Kahlo.* Albuquerque: University of New Mexico Press, 1993.

Winter, Jonah, and Jeanette Winter (illustrator). *Diego.* New York: Alfred A. Knopf, 1991.

Wolfe, Bertran D. *The Fabulous Life of Diego Rivera.* Lanham, MD: Scarborough House, 1992.

Zamora, Martha (compiler). *The Letters of Frida Kahlo.* San Francisco: Chronicle Books, 1995.

NOTES

Singing Frogs The midwife dumped me: paraphrase, Marnham, *Dreaming with His Eyes Open*, p. 18. *Tía* Cesaria: Diego claimed that his grandmother picked him up. But most accounts say that his aunt Cesaria, not his grandmother, was present at his birth. **Antonia the Healer** Jaguars: Brenner, *The Boyhood of Diego Rivera*, p. 22. Tarascan Indian melodies: Ibid., p. 21. No longer scrawny: Rivera and March, *My Art, My Life*, p. 4. **The Engineer** Engineer: Diego was called the Little Engineer. He claimed that when he was four he drove a train. **Devil Diego** *Tía* Vicenta: Diego's mother's aunt. Templo de San Diego de Alcalá: One of many Catholic churches in Guanajuato. "She's made out": paraphrase, Wolfe, *The Fabulous Life of Diego Rivera*, p. 19. "The devil is in him!": paraphrase, Rivera and March, *My Art, My Life*, p. 6. **The Sound of Life** Moved to Mexico: Diego's mother moved her children from Guanajuato because her husband— a freemason and liberal opponent of the president, Porfirio Díaz—was being pursued by the Church and the government. Diego's father followed his family to Mexico City. Dressed like a priest: Rivera Marín, *Diego Rivera the Red*, p. 80. Another, and another: Diego spent three months at the Colegio del Padre Antonio; a report card for August 1895 shows him a bright student at the Colegio Católico Carpenter; a report card dated December 1896 shows him at the Liceo Católico Hispano-Mexicano. Father Servin: Director of the Liceo Católica Hispano-Mexicano. A French teacher: Ernesto Ledoyen, a former officer of the French army and a Communist. **On the Road to Becoming an Artist** José Guadalupe Posada: 1852-1906, Mexican engraver and illustrator. Diego claimed he met Posada, the most important of his teachers, but some biographers say that there is no evidence that Diego apprenticed with Posada and that Diego might have borrowed the story from fellow muralist José Clemente Orozco. Force of feeling: Rivera and March, *My Art, My Life*, p. 18. *La Catrina*: In 1947-1948 Diego painted his mural, *Dream of a Sunday Afternoon in the Alameda Park*, in which Posada's *Catrina* and Posada himself appear. Shocking-pink socks: Rivera Marín, *Un río, dos Riveras*, p. 32. **Passage of Anger** Mill owners treating workers like beasts: paraphrase, Rivera and March, *My Art, My Life*, p. 24. Porfirio Díaz: 1830-1915, president of Mexico from 1876 until 1880 and again from 1884 until 1911; he was a dictator who gave away the land of poor peasants to wealthy landowners. "Father of His People": Rivera and March, *My Art, My Life*, p. 24. I wanted to join them: Diego claimed he put aside his brushes and fought with the mill workers. He might have been in the area when the strike started but, according to biographer Patrick Marnham, the riot didn't start until early 1907, when Diego was already in Spain. Railway flatcars: Marnham, *Dreaming with His Eyes Open*, p. 48. **No More Cézannes** Cézanne: 1839-1906, Diego Rivera wanted to meet Paul Cézanne, but the French artist died a few months before Rivera left for Spain. *Card Players*: Rivera and March, *My Art, My Life*, p. 33. "I have no more": Ibid. **Diego Diegovich** Angelina Beloff: 1879-1969, Russian engraver, painter, and illustrator of children's books, and Diego Rivera's partner for ten years. She died in Mexico City. "My love for you": Rivera Marín, *Diego Rivera the Red*, p. 136. Lenin: 1870-1924, Vladimir Ilyich Lenin, a Russian Communist. Trotsky: 1879-1940. In 1902, Russian leader Lev Davidovich Bronstein changed his name to Leon Trotsky. "Our country is so": Rivera Marín, *Diego Rivera the Red*, p. 138. "I foresee": Ibid., p.145. "For that reason": paraphrase, Ibid., p. 146. "The reason": Ibid. "To reflect in peace": Hamill, *Diego Rivera*, p. 37. **The Mexican Revolution** Porfirio Díaz's wife: Carmen Romero Rubio de Díaz purchased six of Diego's painting and arranged for the government to buy another seven. Emiliano Zapata: 1879-1919. A leading figure in the Mexican Revolution against the dictatorship of Porfirio Díaz. **Behold the Angel** Heading for Paris!: Rivera Marín, *Diego Rivera the Red*, p. 197. **Mexican Cubism** I never believed in God: Wolfe, *The Fabulous Life of Diego Rivera*, p. 107. Picasso: 1881-1973, Pablo Picasso, Spanish painter renowned for his cubism, was a friend of Diego Rivera's until—according to Diego—Picasso plagiarized a painting by Rivera. **World War I Baby** "If the child disturbs me": Wolfe, *The Fabulous*

Life of Diego Rivera, p. 99. Dieguito: Diego Miguel Angel Rivera y Beloff. It was cold: Ibid., p. 100. **Good-byes** I loved love more: paraphrase, Hamill, *Diego Rivera*, p. 75. My wretched and exuberant: Wolfe, *The Fabulous Life of Diego Rivera*, p. 121. **Savage Beauty** *The Creation*: Diego Rivera's mural at the National Preparatory School in Mexico City. Her hair: Rivera and March, *My Art, My Life*, p. 74. "Is *this* the great Diego Rivera?": Ibid. Her hands: Ibid. Her full lips: Ibid. Animal teeth: Ibid. "Shall I model for you?": paraphrase, Ibid., p.75. Lupe: Guadalupe "Lupe" Marín married Diego Rivera in church. The Mexican government didn't recognize a church marriage. **True Mexico** The poetry of the common people: Rivera and March, *My Art, My Life*, p. 41. Hopes, fears: Ibid., p. 19. "Horrible expensive": Rivera Marín, *Un río, dos Riveras*, p. 154. **The Making of a Fresco** I studied: Rivera and March, *My Art, My Life*, p.79. "Scrape it all off": paraphrase, Wolfe, *The Fabulous Life of Diego Rivera*, p. 181. Seven days a week: Rivera and March, *My Art, My Life*, p. 80. My vision of the truth: Ibid., p. 79. **Brimming with Mexican Light** As naturally: Diego was painting *A Cosmography of Modern Mexico* in the Ministry of Education in Mexico City. Clearer, richer: Rivera and March, *My Art, My Life*, p. 72. **Fecund Earth** Chapingo: *The Liberated Land* is the unifying theme of the mural at the *Universidad Autónoma de Chapingo*. The end wall panel, *The Liberated Earth with Natural Forces Controlled by Man*, has Lupe representing Fecund Earth. **Wild Wife** "When you come back": Rivera Marín, *Un río, dos Riveras*, p. 199. Poet: Mexican Jorge Cuesta (1903-1942) was born in Córdova, Veracruz. **Wings of a Blackbird** "Diego, come down!": Wolfe, *The Fabulous Life of Diego Rivera*, p. 243. "I want you to tell me": Rivera and March, *My Art, My Life*, p. 102. "I would appreciate": Wolfe, *The Fabulous Life of Diego Rivera*, p. 243. She must continue to paint: paraphrase, Rivera and March, *My Art, My Life*, p. 103. "I live in Coyoacán": Ibid. Frida Kahlo: 1907-1954. The Mexican painter renowned for her self-portraits. She married Diego Rivera in court, the only legal marriage Diego had had up until then. **Devil Frida** Frida's father: German photographer Wilhelm (Guillermo) Kahlo. "She is a devil.": Rivera and March, *My Art, My Life*, p. 104. The happiest day: paraphrase, Ibid., p. 102. **An Orchid for Frida** Detroit: Diego went first to California, where he painted his mural *Allegory of California* in the Luncheon Club of the Pacific Stock Exchange in San Francisco; *Still Life and Blossoming Almond Trees* at the University of California at Berkeley, Stern Hall; and *The Making of a Fresco, Showing the Building of a City* in the San Francisco Art Institute. *Detroit Industry* is Diego's mural at the Detroit Institute of Arts. **Man at the Crossroads** Man at the Crossroads: Diego Rivera's destroyed mural at Rockefeller Center was entitled *Man at the Crossroads Looking with Hope and High Vision to the Choosing of a New and Better Future*. In 1934 he painted a revised version—*Man, Controller of the Universe*—in the Museo de Bellas Artes in Mexico City. Man and machine: Rivera and March, *My Art, My Life*, p. 112. Peasant who develops: Helms, *Diego Rivera: A Retrospective*, p. 295. Nelson Rockefeller: 1908-1979. American politician, philanthropist, businessman, and governor of New York from 1959 to 1973. **Volcanic Love** Cristina: Cristina Kahlo was Frida's youngest sister. Frida took a lover. She had a brief affair with Russian leader Leon Trotsky (1879-1940) whom Diego had brought to Mexico. **Anguish and Triumph** What sort of a man was I?: Rivera and March, *My Art, My Life*, p. 180. San Francisco: Diego was painting the mural *Pan-American Unity (Marriage of the Artistic Expression of the North and South of This Continent)* for the Golden Gate International Exposition. Today the mural is in the lobby of City College of San Francisco's art auditorium. **Frida's Words** Paraphrase, excerpts from "Portrait of Diego," Tibol, *An Open Life*, pp.137-154. **Diego's Words** I don't blame people: Wolfe, *The Fabulous Life of Diego Rivera*, p. 360. No artist in Mexico: Herrera, *Frida*, p. 361. Her art is acid and tender: Wolfe, *The Fabulous Life of Diego Rivera*, p. 360. Never before has a woman: Rivera and March, *My Art, My Life*, p. 124. Everything that interests me: paraphrase, Marnham, *Dreaming with His Eyes Open*, p. 308. **Still Lifes** Whose last painting had watermelons cut open like her: Frida's last painting was *¡Viva la vida! Long Live Life!* (1954). Diego's last painting: *The Watermelons* (1957). **Epilogue** "Take from life all it gives you": Wolfe, *The Fabulous Life of Diego Rivera*, p. 359. **The True Life of Diego Rivera** "He's just a child": Wolfe, *The Fabulous Life of Diego Rivera*, p. 251. "Do you want to see": paraphrase, Ibid., p. 239.

IN HIS OWN WORDS

"For me painting and life are one. It is my dominant passion." Wolfe, *The Fabulous Life of Diego Rivera*, p. 128.

"The best I have done grew out of things deeply felt, the worst from a pride in mere talent." Rivera and March, *My Art, My Life*, p. 18.

"A vision of my vocation—to produce true and complete pictures of the life of the toiling masses." Rivera and March, *My Art, My Life*, p. 40.

"When you say 'America' you refer to the territory stretching between the icecaps of the two poles." Marnham, *Dreaming with His Eyes Open*, p. 238.

"The peasant and urban folk produce not only grains and vegetables and industrial artifacts, but also beauty." Wolfe, *The Fabulous Life of Diego Rivera*, p. 146.

"In human creation there is something which belongs to humanity at large, and no individual owner has the right to destroy it or keep it solely for his own enjoyment." Rivera and March, *My Art, My Life*, p. 129.

"He who hopes to be universal in his art must plant its own soil. Great art is like a tree that grows in a particular place and has a trunk, leaves, blossoms, boughs, fruit, and roots of its own. The more native art is, the more it belongs to the entire world, because taste is rooted in nature. When art is true, it is one with nature. This is the secret of primitive art and also of the art of the masters—Michelangelo, Cézanne, Seurat, and Renoir. The secret of my best work is that it is Mexican." Rivera and March, *My Art, My Life*, p. 31.